RAFAEL NADAL

An Unauthorized Biography

eISBN: 9781619841741

ISBN: 9781619843790

RAFAEL NADAL

An Unauthorized Biography

BELMONT&
BELCOURT

Table of Contents

Greatness Doesn't Have a Minimum Age 11

Rafael Becomes "Rafa" 23

Pathway To The Top 29

Beyond the Court 65

Sweat escapes his saturated headband and falls to the lush grass surface. His hand tightens around the vinyl grip of his trusted tennis racket. Soon, he will be known across the globe as the youngest Wimbledon player to have ever made it this far, but he must first find a weakness in his formidable opponent, who stares at him from across the majestic court.

Fans watching this grueling match become a distant sound in the background as all of his focus is now on the task at hand. His eyes block out all distractions as he awaits the mighty serve from the other side of the court. He has quickly become acquainted with what awaits him.

Unnoticed by his fans and his opponent, this champion of the court soon discovers a slight weakness in his opponent that he might be able to capitalize on to launch himself into the next round. It is such a slight weakness to the eye that many may not even notice, but his training has allowed him to notice such traits, and his skill has allowed him to use that weakness to gain the slight advantage that all players seek.

His opponent's red face, profuse sweating and heavy breathing all point to one particular weakness that Nadal can use in his favor—fatigue. The long, grueling match has finally taken its toll on his opponent. He will use his opponent's fatigue to overcome and prevail in this final set.

As the ball is thrown into the air, awaiting the blowing strike from the racket, Rafael Nadal knows this match is now his. A slight grin crosses his face, which is matched by the growing confidence that resides within him.

Belmont and Belcourt Biographies

"He has never broken a racket in anger. It would be showing a lack of respect to people who actually have to buy the equipment to play the sport."

— Uncle Toni Nadal on nephew, Rafael

Greatness Doesn't Have a Minimum Age

When the clock struck midnight on June 3, 1986 in Manacor, Majorca, Spain, the world was not yet aware that one of the best tennis players of all time was preparing to make his way into the world. Later that day, Sebastian Nadal and Ana Maria Parera would welcome their first child, Rafael Nadal, into their family.

A few short years later, the Nadal family would welcome their second child, Maria Isabel, into the world. Rafael would become a big brother. The Nadal family was close-knit, and would remain strong throughout Rafael's soon-to-be discovered fame and fortune. Due to the creation of a strong family base, the Nadals still live together in their family home located in Manacor, Spain.

One would assume that Rafael would follow his father, Sebastian, into the business world. Considering that Sebastian Nadal owns Vidres Mallorca, which is a glass and window company, and also manages his own restaurant, Sa Punta, the son following the father would come naturally, and Rafael would have all the knowledge and opportunity that his father had. It would be quite simple for Rafael to work alongside his father, Sebastian, and one day take over one or both of his father's businesses; however, fate and Rafael had other plans for this future tennis Hall of Famer.

Sports ran in the Nadal family and didn't steer far from Rafael. His uncle played professional soccer and another uncle was a professional tennis player. He definitely had options within the sporting world.

His Uncle Miguel Angel Nadal was a retired soccer player who had played for RCD Mallorca, the Spanish National Team, and FC Barcelona, which led Rafael to supporting soccer clubs such as Real Madrid and his Uncle's old team, RCD Mallorca. Rafael's love of soccer has never left him, and he played soccer extensively as a child and showed much skill with the game. Indeed, his Uncle Miguel's talents landed directly upon young Rafael, and it showed on the soccer field. From the onset, it was apparent that he was faster, more agile, and more athletically gifted than the other children on the field, and his never-ending energy made him a great threat to the other team later in the match. It seemed that Rafael would become one of the best soccer players in the world.

However, Rafael's Uncle Toni Nadal was also a sports star in his own right and wanted to show Rafael another sport to choose. A former professional tennis player, his Uncle Toni had recognized that Rafael showed a natural gift for the sport at a very early age. When Uncle Toni took his nephew, Rafael, to his first tennis court at the tender age of three, Rafael took the tennis racket and knew almost instinctively how to hold it, how to swing it, and what to do with it. From that point forward, Uncle Toni took the young Rafael under his wing and began showing him how to play the game that he loved.

At just eight years old, Rafael entered an Under-12 Regional Tournament. He would go on to win that tournament, and it would be the first glimpse of what Rafael could accomplish on the court. After that tournament, his Uncle Toni knew that Rafael had the potential to be someone special within the tennis world. He would soon intensify Rafael's tennis lessons and persuade him to switch his style to that of a left-hander. The change would give Rafael an advantage against his opponents and would prevent him from making two-handed forehand swings.

When Rafael turned twelve years old, he found himself the winner of both the Spanish and European tennis titles within his age group. He played soccer and tennis so much that his schoolwork suffered.

Having two superstar uncles in two separate sports and a father that was a very successful businessman who thought highly of education, Rafael had many options to choose from at a very young age; however, Rafael was a typical child and just wanted to play. He wanted to play any sport. Coupled with his unstoppable energy, Rafael decided to play both tennis and soccer. Why not? He had the uncles to show him all they knew, he had the natural athletic ability to be great in either sport, and was a child with a very supportive family.

For these reasons, Rafael would play both sports simultaneously until his father would make him chose just one. Sebastian did not want his son's education to suffer further because of the hectic requirements needed to keep up with two sports. Around the age of twelve, Rafael had to decide on which sport to pursue. This choice was a difficult one for the young Rafael to make. He loved tennis and soccer and wished to play them both; however, he understood his father's concerns about his education and knew he had to make a choice. At this point, he decided to stick with tennis and become only a fan of the soccer game—a decision that would prove to be a very solid choice for him.

When he turned fourteen years old, the Spanish Tennis Federation made a request to the Nadal family. They suggested that Rafael move to Barcelona in order to continue his training. If Rafael and his family agreed, he would be provided with more financial assistance toward his tennis career. The family rejected this idea. The decision was based primarily upon his family's fear that Rafael's education would be held back due to moving to Barcelona. Secondly, Uncle Toni mentioned to the family that he refused to believe that you can't become a great champion by moving to another place. He believed that you could become great without ever leaving your home.

Had they agreed to it, the move would have meant that the family would receive financial help for Rafael's tennis lessons;

however, the offer didn't get them to move away from home. Sebastian decided to pay for all of his son's tennis lessons and equipment himself. His family immensely supported this decision and they made adjustments in their lifestyles as needed. Rafael would be Manacor's home-grown champion, and had all the support he would ever need.

In May of 2001, he would find himself at a clay court exhibition match against the former Grand Slam Champion, Pat Cash. Pat Cash had originally been scheduled to play Boris Becker. The match had to be rearranged due to a scheduling conflict with Boris Becker, and Pat Cash was not happy about facing the young tennis phenomenon. Rafael went on to win the match by a narrow margin, showing the tennis world that he was the real deal.

Later that same year, when Rafael turned fifteen, he would become a professional tennis player. At the 2001 Seville Challenger, Rafael's first match as a professional tennis player, he would be victorious. Having a taste of success on the professional level gave him the momentum to go on and defeat Ramon Delgado in the opening round at a Masters-Level match in

Manacor. Rafael would be the ninth player to win a match before his sixteenth birthday during the Open Era and give him a world ranking of 762.

That year saw Rafael play in nine events on the Futures Circuit. Within those nine events, he won six tournaments. All of them were held in Spain. He would go on to reach the semifinals of a Challengers event in Barcelona while also reaching the semi-finals on a Junior Tournament held at Wimbledon. That year, he was also dubbed *El Niño*, or child. If you found your name next to the *El Niño*, you knew you would have your hands full throughout the match.

It didn't take long before word spread about Rafael's "never-say-die" playing style. The longer a player kept Rafael in a match, the harder he was to defeat. Even though every swing from his tennis racket would have a tremendous amount of energy behind it, Rafael never seemed to tire out or show signs of fatigue. This proved to be a daunting task to any player that faced him. His weakness on the court was so minimal that opposing players found it difficult to use those flaws to gain an advantage.

If you didn't quickly put the game out of reach of Rafael, he would eventually come back to defeat you.

This playing style, along with the signature biting of the trophy and his own unique tennis apparel, made him a quick favorite amongst tennis fans. It was clear from the beginning that the tennis world was quickly becoming Rafael's world, and he was just getting started.

"He is like a beast, an animal, on the court. He's very strong, and he's very well prepared."

— Guillermo Coria after losing to Rafael Nadal in Monte Carlo

Rafael Becomes "Rafa"

Even though Rafael had turned professional in 2001 and was victorious in many matches, he still held the moniker of *El Niño*. That nickname wouldn't last long: as the 2003 season began, he would climb his way toward the number one position in the world of tennis. Up to this point, he hadn't moved up nor down very much within the world player standings. With the opening of the 2003 ATP season, that would change, and Rafael would begin to make his climb toward the top.

His first step toward the number one player position was with impressive victories within the first four Challenger events of the year. Racking up wins against quality players such as Karol Kucera, Albert Costa and Carlos Moya—just to name a few—the name "Rafael Nadal" was quickly becoming well-known by that spring. Word about Rafael's style of "never say die" play spread like wildfire with the players, and any player who found himself or herself matched-up against Rafael knew that it was going to be a long day.

Rafael's style of play not only impressed players he would find himself matched up against, but it would often win over crowds who watched him in amazement. Diving for a return that would prove to stun his opponent for a win, returning a shot from well behind the baseline for a win when it appeared he was merely trying to survive his opponents onslaught, or a simple drop shot just over the net during a hard-returning match made the crowds watch in awe at their newly found favorite tennis player. This style of play is an exciting and oftentimes heart-stopping style that brings both new and longtime tennis fans to the court.

Rafael isn't just a phenomenon on the court. His off-court style is just as awe-inspiring. He has brought a tennis clothing style to the court that has never been seen before. With his outlandishly colored shirts, his capris-style shorts, and that signature headband, he is leading the charge on what "tennis style" is. Anyone can clearly see that he not only wants to have fun while playing tennis, he wants to have fun dressing for tennis.

Rafael has also inspired a new celebratory method after a tournament victory by biting the winning trophy. No one knows why he does this, but it is clear that it is his own unique style that he wants the world to see.

The last personality trait that has turned "Rafael" into "Rafa" for fans is his simple lifestyle. He still lives with his mother, father and sister in his childhood town of Manacor and still roots for all the childhood sports teams that he once did. Nothing much has changed for Rafa except that he is now a little more famous — a quote which he has made on more than a few occasions.

All of these characteristics combined make one of the most exciting players the tennis world has ever seen. He has definitely won the title of the "Fans Champion." He has also won the right to be called "Rafa."

"I am afraid of a lot of things. A dog. I could be afraid of a dog that's upset, for example. And on the tennis courts, maybe on the outside I look fearless, but on the inside, I'm scared. There's not one player in the world who isn't nervous before matches. Especially important matches"

−Rafael Nadal

Pathway To The Top

After his wins in the opening part of the 2003 season, Rafa had a slight setback. It appeared that he would take the French Open by storm due to the slow, red clay court. His two-handed backswing delivered such a tremendous spin on the ball that many opponents didn't know how to handle it. Often, that spin would be the defining game-winning return of the match.

However, the court had different plans for Rafa this time. While practicing prior to the tournament start, he strained his elbow and had to drop out from the tournament. He had no choice but to watch the tournament from the sidelines and not participate.

After a quick recovery, he was able to play at Wimbledon that year, where he went on to defeat Mario Ancic and Simon Childs before losing to Paradorn Srichapan. That advancement marked the first time a player as young as Rafa had advanced so far at the All England Club since Boris Becker did it in 1984.

Wimbledon also marked the only grass court tournament that Rafa had played on in all of the 2003 season. His forehand shots didn't have the topspin kick that it had on clay courts, but his sideline-to-sideline playing style made up for that lack. The only other advantage he had on this grass court was the sliding return shots he made that forced his opponents to return uncomfortable volleys.

Later in the 2003 season, he played at an event in Croatia. He made it to the semifinals in this Masters Tournament, a feat he had not previously accomplished. It also marked his first ever ATP Tour victory by winning a doubles tournament with partner Lopez Moron. At the end of the 2003 season, Rafa found himself the 47th ranked player in the tennis world. Considering he started a few short seasons ago in the shadows of relative obscurity (762nd), Rafa finished the season as a very formidable player who had a bright future ahead of him.

Part of this drastic improvement not only lied in the advanced skill he had formed, but also because his body had matured tremendously over that course of time. He had gotten stronger, filled out his muscles and never lost any flexibility or agility. He basically lost nothing and gained everything, which made him a fiercer competitor on the court—a player who not only had the knowledge and skills to get a job done, but the strength to back him up.

At the opening of the 2004 season in Auckland, New Zealand, Rafa put on a great show of athleticism. He reached the finals for singles competition for the first time in his fledgling career. Unfortunately, at that singles final, he would ultimately lose to Domink Hrbaty. He went on to the Australia Open and made a good showing by reaching the third round. He would go on to lose to Lleyton Hewitt at the end of that round.

Spain's Davis Cup Team enlisted Rafa to play for them. He rewarded Spain's confidence by taking the fifth and decisive match against the Czech Republic by defeating their player, Radek Stepanek, which enabled his fellow countrymen to advance. During that time, he would also partner up with Tommy Robredo three times in doubles play, however, victory would only find the double team once during those three outings.

Later in the season, Rafa would once again show his greatness to Spain by winning the deciding match against France.

This would pit Spain against the United States in the Davis Cup finals. Rafa would place Spain in the victory column by a score of 3-2. He defeated Andy Roddick in four sets and became the youngest player in history to win a finals match as a player of the winning squad.

A match that time would prove to be a great rivalry came in Miami of that year. It matched Rafa against Roger Federer, an unknown rival at the time that would renew the public's interest in men's tennis. Rafa had earned the trait of being a "grinder," while Federer was known as an "artist." This match-up brought up comparisons to the great Ali-Fraser fight in the boxing world. Muhammad Ali was known as the boxing "artist," while Joe Frasier was known as the "grinder." That rivalry renewed an interest in the boxing world just as the Federer-Rafa rivalry could do.

In the match, Rafa gave everything he had to Federer. Federer simply didn't know how to handle this upcoming tennis superstar. Rafa grinded it out and the match went the distance, with Rafa coming out victorious. Needless to say, this victory shocked the tennis world and propelled Rafa to become a household name almost overnight.

Their battle on the court wasn't the only reason this rivalry would become one of the greatest rivalries in the tennis world. The two men were just as different off the court as on the court. Federer was a more refined, traditional tennis player in every way in comparison to Rafa, from the clothes he wore to the humble acceptance of the trophies he earned. Rafa was a more charismatic player who offered a tremendous amount of energy while playing. Rafa's clothes were not just a fashion statement he was attempting to make; they reflected his approach to the game—fun and carefree. Even his method of celebrating after a tournament win by biting the trophy was something tennis had never seen. He was as different from Federer as one could imagine, which only fueled the rivalry to greatness.

The French Open would be the next tournament Rafa would look forward to attending. At the last season's French Open, he put on quite a show and was making his mark as being "King of the Clay Courts." However, fate had other plans for Rafa. A stress fracture in his ankle sidelined him for several months. He would not only miss the French Open, he would also miss out on his chance for a return at Wimbledon.

Rafael reflected his trademark "never say die" attitude by him returning to good health by the end of the season and winning his first-ever singles championship in Sopot, Poland. Even with the injuries of the season, Rafa went on to play in 17 tournaments and the Davis Cup. Due to the injuries, he would finish the season as the 51st rank player in the tennis world—a drop from the previous year's finish of 47th.

No other year had such a tremendous effect on Rafa's tennis career than the season of 2005. Many would consider the 2005 season to be Rafa's "breakout" season by surpassing Mats Wilander's record of wins by a teenager. Wilander's previous record of nine tournament wins by a teenager was beaten by Rafa's record of eleven tournament wins, including the French Open. Other tournament wins for Rafa that year included Stuttgart, Beijink, Madrid, Montreal, Rome, Barcelona, Bastad and Monte Carlo. He also placed one in the win column as a Doubles Titles in Doha, India.

The 2005 season also showed a rematch of the rivalry between Rafa and Federer. Once again, the match came in a tournament, in Miami. The match-up came during the finals. It was the first time these two great tennis stars would meet on such a lofty level; however, the victory would go to Federer during this encounter. It took quite some time for Federer to vanquish Rafa, appearing at times that he had difficulty trying to find a weakness in Rafa's game. At one point, Rafa had Federer down by two sets, only for Federer to come back and win the tournament. The match lasted for five sets before the Swiss tennis star could capture the victory over this young talk of tennis.

Even in the loss, Rafa's ranking skyrocketed, finally breaking into the top 20 in the world rankings. At the end of April, Rafa would eventually crack the top 10, a place he had once only dreamed about.

The longest match Rafa had to face came in that year when he met up with Coria during a tournament held in Rome. The pair of Spaniards fought back and forth for five hours and fourteen minutes before Rafa overcame Coria for the win. This match also set the record for the longest final match during the Open Era. If it weren't for Rafa's relentless energy level and "never say die" style of play, this match would have gone to Coria fairly quickly; however, Rafa's natural instinct to win led him down the path to victory. This match is another example of what turns Rafael into "Rafa" on the court.

When the time came for the French Open, Rafa's winning streak didn't end. He appeared to be unstoppable. He ripped through opponents such as Richard Gasquet, Sebastien Grosjean and David Ferrer. He would once again face his nemesis, Roger Federer, in the semi-finals, were he would down him and go on to face Mariano Puerta in the finals. The clay court that the French Open offered proved to be the perfect surface for Rafa. He defeated all who faced him and went on to win the entire tournament. The French Open also allowed Rafa to make a couple of more marks in the history books with his name beside them. It was the first time a player had won a Grand Slam since Wilander accomplished it in 1982, and Rafa was the first teenager to win a title at Roland Garros since Michael Chang won it. Indeed, Rafa put the tennis world on notice that he was here, and was the real deal.

He wrapped up the season by posting two more tournament wins and settling himself in the ATP's #2 World Ranking of Players. He once again placed his name in the record books by being the first Spanish player to be ranked that high at the end of the year.

By looking at his statistics that year that allowed him to capture the number two position in the world rankings, one can see that once his opponent would serve the ball to Rafa, they would be playing defense for the rest of the match. He led the tour in many areas: points won returning first serve was 37%; points won returning second serve was 57%; and games won on return was 38%. He ranked 4th in the tour with break points converted at 46%. The most glowing example of his skills came in the form of tournament money won. He won the most money ever by a teenager, with a total purse for the season of $3.8 million. This was not bad, considering he stayed at his hometown for training. This just proved to the world that his Uncle Toni had it right by saying a player doesn't need to leave home to become great at what he does.

The 2006 season didn't go so well for Rafa. He only won five tournaments but did repeat as the French Open Champion. Some may say that even though he only had five tournament wins, Rafa still had a solid 2006 outing because he held on to the

#2 spot in the world rankings. He also didn't lose a single match on a clay court and retained his "King of the Clay Court" moniker. Additionally, he advanced his play at Wimbledon to demonstrate that he was also capable of great play on grass courts.

One could only surmise that 2006 was still a solid year for the young Rafa predominately because he met with his archrival, Federer, five times during that season and won four of the meet-ups. The only loss that Rafa would feel at the hands of Federer would be at Wimbledon in the finals—thus fueling the rivalry even further between the two tennis greats.

The greatest of the matches between Rafa and Federer came in Rome. The match lasted for five hours and five minutes—just short of the record amount of time Rafa and his opponent Caria had played at the same court the year prior. Federer dominated Rafa for most of the match, with Rafa struggling to stay in the match; however, just as Rafa had demonstrated so often in other matches, if you don't put the match away early, Rafa will eventually come back for the win. This match was no different. Federer couldn't put Rafa away early, so he was able to come back for the victory.

That match not only was another great match-up between the rivals, but it also marked Rafa's 16th tournament win as a teenager. That record had not been matched since Bjorn Borg set it in the mid 1970's.

Rafa had not lost a single tournament final since his meet-up with Federer the season prior in Miami. Federer changed that streak when the two faced each other at Wimbledon in the 2006 season. Rafa was entering the tournament with back pain, but he had played so well, and had not mentioned anything about an injury, that nobody realized his back had been giving him problems. He served 80 times throughout the tournament prior to facing Federer once again. Federer broke Rafa's serve in the first game. He went on to defeat Rafa within four sets.

The 2007 season would begin see Rafa add one more tournament victory to his prior year's total. With wins at Monte Carlo, Stuttgard, Roland Garros, Barcelona, Rome and Indian Wells, the 2007 season would give him a total of six tournament wins. One of the wins was once again against Roger Federer at the French Open within four sets. Prior to that win, Federer put an end to Rafa's 81-match winning streak on a clay court. He defeated Rafa in Hamburg, which not only handed Rafa a loss, but it was his first loss on a clay court. The loss to Federer not only ended a massive clay court winning streak, but also ended a 2007 winning streak on a clay court that included a victory in straight sets over Federer in Monte Carlo.

The greatest match of the season came between Federer and Rafa at Wimbledon. Even though Federer would become victorious over the course of the five exciting sets, he would walk away from the tournament not really knowing anything about Rafa's game. Rafa, on the other hand, would come away from that tournament with more knowledge about Federer's grass court game. Experts argued that the tennis world was beginning to see a changing of the guard when it came to the number one player in the world. Why not? There was ample evidence that Rafa was indeed worthy of the top spot. Considering he had dominated all opponents on clay surfaces and now was gaining more skills on grass surfaces, the choice should have been clear. The typical grass surface was where Roger Federer would find a way to become victorious over Rafa. It was Federer's only method to level the playing field when facing Rafa. If Rafa could find a way to dominate the grass courts, there was no other player in the game today that could handle what Rafa had to give them. Thus, Rafa would be recognized as the number one player in the world, and rightly so.

Rafa would finish the season still holding the number two position in the rankings, right on Federer's heels at number one position. Despite Rafa being the only player to top 30 wins on both clay and hard court surfaces, he would not see the number one position for the 2007 season. Federer was a great player in his own right, and he had a firm grasp of the number one slot in the rankings. It was clear that Rafa would have to remove Federer from the throne of number one and Federer would not give it up easily.

He opened the 2008 season by advancing himself to the semi-finals in the Australian Open. He appeared to be in typical Rafa form throughout the opening matches. When he met up against Jo-Wilfried Tsonga, he would face defeat.

Rafa would rebound, however, a few months later at the French Open. He would post his fourth straight French Open Tournament victory by defeating Roger Federer once again. It was also his third win over Federer that spring. The victory not only rewarded Rafa with another win over his rival, it also set up a great match for the Wimbledon fans to witness.

As if to grow the anticipation level from everyone involved and watching, the match was delayed by rain twice, and the match ended around sunset. The total playing time for the five set match-up was four hours and 48 minutes. It marked the longest match in Wimbledon history.

During the match, it appeared that Rafa had Federer beaten by the fourth set, but a few uncommon miscues allowed Federer back into the match. Rafa regrouped himself in the fifth set and beat Federer by a score of 9-7.

Just as Federer had ended Rafa's clay court winning streak, Rafa ended Federer's chances of becoming the first player in over a century to win six straight Wimbledons. Some fans may say that Rafa paid back Federer by handing him a defeat in that Wimbledon tournament. Either way, just as all witnessed Rafa's streak end, we watched Federer's Wimbledon winning streak end.

Later that season, Rafa played for Spain in the Olympics. Rafa would come home victorious for Spain by winning the coveted gold medal in the singles competition. The Olympian effort simply added to "Rafa Mania".

After the Olympics, Rafa finally achieved the number one spot in the world rankings, marking the first time since 1984 that a left-handed player had won such a position. In 1984, John McEnroe, a left-handed player, had held the number one position and had gone on to become one of the most recognizable and best players in tennis history.

He finished the 2008 season by reaching the finals in 10 tournaments and winning eight of them. He led the ATP Tour in points won while receiving first and second serve, the amount of games won while serving and second serve points won while serving. He placed fourth in games won while serving with a tremendous 88%. He ended the season with more than $6.7 million in winnings and sent his career earnings well over $20 million.

The 2009 ATP Tour season opened for Rafa on a tremendous note. The first official ATP Tour Event was in Doah, where he was awarded the 2008 ATP World Tour Champion Trophy. Unfortunately, he would go on to lose in the quarterfinals to Gael Monfils. He bounced back within that tournament to team up with partner Marc Lopez and defeat the number one ranked doubles team of Daniel Nestor and Nenad Zimonjic. This marked the first time since 1980 that a world number one player had played a world number one doubles player within a final.

At the 2009 Australia Open, Rafa defeated a fellow countryman, Fernando Verdasco, in an unbelievable five-hour semifinal match-up and went on to defeat his rival, Roger Federer, in the final match-up. Not only was it a great way to open up the season, it was the first time that a Spaniard had won the Australian Open title and also gave him Grand Slam titles on all three surfaces—clay, grass and hard court. More unbelievable was the fact that it marked the first time a male player had ever held the Aussie, French and Wimbledon championships at the same time.

A side of Rafa that not many had witnessed was on display during the trophy presentation. It was clear that a physically and mentally exhausted Roger Federer was in tears as Rafa hoisted the trophy up to his mouth to perform the signature biting of the trophy. It was at this point that Rafa noticed his fallen rival, visibly broken, and embraced his nemesis to comfort him. Federer welcomed the embrace and showed the rest of the tennis world that there was much more to Rafa than we even thought. The act showed his caring and humble side. Even though he was a standout both on and off the court, it showed he had compassion for his opponents. He keeps this kind of compassion hidden during his match play, but it is a compassion that warrants our utmost respect for the young champion.

Rafa stumbled during the ABN AMRO World Tennis Tournament in Rotterdam. He lost to second seed Murray in three sets. Rafa called his trainer about a tendon problem in his right knee, which clearly affected his play during the match. Although reports indicate that the tendon problem had nothing to do with Rafa's tendonitis, it was severe enough to force him to withdraw from the next tournament at Dubai that was scheduled to take place the following week.

Once he was back to good health, he went on to help Spain defeat Serbia in the Davis Cup World Group first round tie. He defeated Janko Tipsarevic and Novak Djokovic. His defeat of Djokovic marked his twelfth consecutive Davis Cup singles victory and launched him to an 11-4 win/loss record against Djokovic, including a 6-0 record on clay surfaces.

The 2009 Indian Wells Masters was Rafa's thirteenth Masters 1000 Series tournament win and also gave him his first victory over David Nalbandian when he met Nalbandian in the fourth round. He also had victories over Juan Martin del Potro, Andy Roddick and Murray on his way to securing the tournament victory.

During the Miami Masters of that year, Juan Martin del Potro would have redemption against Rafa by defeating him in the quarterfinals, thus knocking him out of the tournament. That victory over Rafa was the first victory for del Potro in five matches against Rafa.

The next tournament for Rafa was the Monte Carlo Masters, where he set another title by defeating Novak Djokovic. The victory would give Rafa his fifth consecutive singles title in that tournament. He also set an ATP Masters Series record by being the only male player to win the same event for five consecutive years.

Rafa went on to set records in Barcelona and Rome by winning those tournaments for five and four consecutive years, respectively. It appeared that no matter where he went in 2009, his play was unstoppable. That is, until he matched-up against his rival Roger Federer in the Madrid Open.

In the Madrid Open, Federer was on top of his game when he met the young Rafa and handed him a loss in the final with a score of 4-6 and 4-6. This was the first time that Rafa would taste defeat at the hands of Federer since the 2007 Tennis Masters Cup.

However, even with the recent loss, the ATP rewarded Rafa by announcing that he was one out of only eight players to qualify for the ATP World Tour Finals. The event was to be held at the O2 Arena located in London, England.

On the heels of the good news from the ATP about the qualification for the O2 Arena, Rafa would once again taste defeat at a location where he had grown accustomed to winning—the French Open. Since 2005, Rafa had been dominating the French Open and laying waste to any player on the other side of the net. After having set a 31 consecutive win streak record, which beat the previous record of 28 held by Bjorn Borg, Rafa's French Open reign would come to an end. Robin Soderling defeated Rafa in the fourth round, thus ending his hopes for a return trip to the trophy.

After the stunning defeat at the French Open, Rafa withdrew from several upcoming tournaments. The first was the AEGON Championships, then Wimbledon, and finally the Davis Cup. After his withdrawal from the AEGON Championships, it was reported that he was suffering from tendonitis in both of his knees. Not making any excuses, one could only assume that this injury had a major influence on his loss at the French Open.

Due to the withdrawals, Rafa dropped to the number two position in the world rankings behind Roger Federer, after Federer won the Wimbledon Title. Rafa would later make a return appearance to the world of tennis at the Rogers Cup in Montreal, Canada.

This return to tennis didn't turn out as Rafa had hoped. He would lose in the quarterfinals to del Potro once again and also lose his number two position in the world rankings, falling to the number three position behind Andy Murray. This marked the first time he would be outside of the top two positions since 2005.

At the U.S. Open, Rafa would hand Fernando Gonzalez a defeat but lose to the eventual champion Juan Martin del Potro. Even with the loss to del Potro, Rafa would regain his number two position in the world rankings and move Andy Murray out of it. Once again, Rafa looked at the number one position from below Federer.

He would finish out the season by helping Spain secure their fourth Davis Cup victory, winning the Golden Bagel Award for 2009 by securing nine 6-0 sets. Rafa had won the Golden Bagel Award three times in his career, which is an ATP Tour record. He would also end the season by securing the number two position in the world rankings. This was the fourth time in five years he would be ranked at that position.

The 2010 season started off on the right note for Rafa when he won the Capitala World Tennis Championship in Abu Dhabi. He defeated David Ferrer and Robin Soderling to secure the win. The season would appear to be on an up and down path after that victory.

He would lose at the Qatar ExxonMobil Open to Nikolay Davydenko and then ultimately lose the Australian Open in the quarterfinals to Andy Murray. During the quarterfinals against Murray, Rafa would pull himself out of the match. Doctors cited more knee injuries and recommended that Rafa take two weeks for rest, and two additional weeks for rehabilitation. Indeed, the injury bug simply kept getting to Rafa's knees and affected his play.

He would once again taste defeat at Indian Wells, but would regain victory in the doubles competition by teaming up with Lopez to defeat Daniel Nestor and Nenad Zimonjic. His doubles ranking would skyrocket 175 places and land at number 66 in the world ranking system.

During a season of ups and downs, Rafa would be defeated once again by Andy Roddick at the Sony Ericsson Open. Rafa regrouped to get back on the winning track at the Monte Carlo Rolex Masters.

He reached his first tour final since Doha earlier in the season by handing David Ferrer a loss in the semifinals. He would go on to victory over Fernando Verdasco to capture the tournament trophy. With the victory, Rafa became the first player in the Open Era to capture a tournament title in six straight years.

For the first time, Rafa elected to sit out on the Barcelona tournament. He would come back, however, and be victorious at Rome by defeating David Ferrer in the finals. This would be the fifth title he had won at Rome, and it tied Andre Agassi's record of 17 ATP Masters Titles.

At the Mutua Madrilena Madrid Open, where he finished as runner-up the previous year, Rafa would defeat Federer and avenge his 2009 finals loss that Federer had handed to him previously. With the Madrid Open Title secured, Rafa would set another record of 18 Masters Titles, a record previously tied by Rafa that Andre Agassi had made with 17. It also marked the first time a player had won all three clay court Masters Titles in a single year, and made Rafa the first player to win three consecutive Masters tournaments—quite an impressive comeback considering how his year had started on an up and down note.

Going into the French Open, fans and reporters alike had hopes of seeing a Rafa/Federer final. This would soon turn to be impossible, for Federer was defeated in the quarterfinals by Robin Soderling. This turned out to be more gratuitous for Rafa than one would think. If he were to win the tournament, it would automatically propel him past Federer in the world rankings and give him the number one position. Rafa would indeed defeat Soderling in the finals and go on, not only win the French Open but to secure the number one position in the world ranking system. With the win, it also gave Rafa his seventh Grand Slam, tying him with tennis superstars such as John McEnroe, John Newcombe and Mats Wilander. The media dubbed this win the "Clay Slam" because Rafa was also the first man to win three Masters Series on clay and the French Open. He also tied a record with Bjorn Borg by winning the French Open without dropping a single set during match play. This also marked the first time a player had won five French Open Titles in six years, and secured Rafa's position in London at the World Tour Finals.

The next tournament on Rafa's schedule was the AEGON Championships, which he had won in 2008. The story wouldn't be the same this season. He would be defeated in the quarterfinals by Feliciano Lopez.

Wimbledon would frown, then smile at Rafa once again. He was fined $2,000 during his match against Petzschner for sideline coaching. It seems that his coach, Uncle Toni, was found to be shouting words of encouragement to Rafa from the sidelines and the Wimbledon officials believed this form of "encouragement" was some sort of code word for giving him sideline coaching during the match. That did not dampen Rafa's competitive spirit, however. He went on to defeat Tomas Berdych in straight sets and win the Wimbledon Title. The win marked his second Wimbledon Title and his eighth career Major Title. He also won the Old World Title. This title had been won by Bjorn Borg in 1978 and can only be won by winning the Italian Open, the French Open and the Wimbledon Titles all in the same year.

He would follow-up the Wimbledon victory with a defeat at the Rogers Cup at the hands of Andy Murray. He would once again play doubles with Djokovic but lose in the first round to Milos Raonic and Vasek Pospisil. The Cincinnati Masters had granted him the top seed spot, but he would lose in the quarterfinals to Marcos Baghdatis.

Rafa would redeem himself once again at the U.S. Open, where he would defeat Novak Djokovic and complete the Career Grand Slam. This victory not only gave him the U.S. Open Title, but also made him the only man to complete the Career Golden

Slam next to Andre Agassi. Rafa was also the only man ever to win Grand Slams on clay, grass and hard court all within the same year and the first to win the French Open, Wimbledon and U.S. Open in the same year since Rod Laver did it in 1969. Rafa also clinched the number one world ranking, making him only the third player ever to regain the number one position after losing it at the beginning of the year. This was a tribute to the never say die attitude that he played with on the court.

After the U.S. Open, his next stop was at the PTT Thailand Open, where he would lose to Guillermo Garcia Lopez. He would once again compose himself and go on to win the next event. At the Rakuten Japan Open Tennis Championships, he comfortably defeated Gael Monfils for his seventh title of the season.

Rafa would lose the next tournament event. At the Shanghai Rolex Masters, Jurgen Melzer defeated Rafa in the third round and snapped his record streak of 21 consecutive Masters quarterfinal appearances. He announced on November 5th that he would pull himself out of the Paris Masters, citing tendinitis in his left shoulder. Rafa would be rewarded the Stefan Edberg Sportsmanship Award in London on November 21st of that year.

This was the first time he would win such an award for sportsmanship.

Rafa would close out his season by being defeated by his rival, Roger Federer, at the ATP World Tour Finals. This would be only the second time of the season that the two rivals would face each other, and Federer would come out victorious. Rafa made no excuses for his loss, only stating that Roger Federer played better than he did on that day. Now we know why he won the Sportsmanship award in London.

Rafa would wrap up the season by posting three Grand Slam victories, three Masters 1000 Tournament victories, and regaining his number one position within the world rankings. He would honor his rival at the end of the year by agreeing to play in two exhibition matches for the Roger Federer Foundation. The first match took place in Zurich and the second match was to be played in Madrid.

The 2011 season started out great for Rafa. He defeated his rival, Federer, at the Mubadala World Tennis Championship in Abu Dhabi; however, fever would strike Rafa at the Qatar ExxonMobil Open in Doha and he would fall to Nikolay Davydenko in the semifinals. He would regain himself and go on with partner Lopez to win the doubles titles by defeating Daniele Bracciali and Andreas Seppi.

During the Australian Open, Rafa appreared to be in great shape. He defeated Marcos Daniel, Ryan Sweeting, Bernard Tomic and Marin Cilic on his way to a quarterfinals matchup against David Ferrer. An apparent hamstring injury to Rafa earlier in the match aided Ferrer in ultimately defeating Rafa. The injury ended Rafa's aspirations to win four major tournaments in a row.

The Laureus World Sportsman of the Year Award went to Rafa for the first time in his career. He was picked ahead of soccer superstar Lionel Messi, Sebastian Vettel, Andres Iniesta, Los Angeles Lakers NBA star Kobe Bryant, and Filipino boxing sensation Manny Pacquiao.

Once again, Rafa would help Spain at the Davis Cup. He would defeat Ruben Bemelmans and Olivier Rochus to secure the victory.

He would go on to make a good showing at Indian Wells that year. Rafa would make it to the finals, but eventually lose to

Novak Djokovic in the final round. The next day, Rafa and Djokovic decided to play a friendly match in Colombia. Rafa would come out victorious and regain some pride.

The following week at the Sony Ericsson Open in Miami, Rafa would easily walk through the competition until the quarterfinals, where he was matched up against the number seven world ranked player, Tomas Berdych. He played well during the first set, but had an apparent shoulder injury strike him in the second set. He lost the second set but came back to win the third—another testament to the tenaciousness of his play.

He would face his rival, Federer, in the semifinal, and it was the first semifinal meeting of the two rivals since the 2007 Masters Cup. Rafa handled Federer with ease and it was one of the fastest matches played on the hard court. For the second time in two weeks, he would meet-up with rising rival Novak Djokovic in the finals. Once again, Rafa would fall to Djokovic in a thrilling three-set tiebreaker. This finals appearance also marked the first time that Rafa had made it to the finals at Indian Wells and Miami in the same year.

The following win at the Monte Carlo Rolex Masters gave Rafa his 19th Masters Titles, his 44th career title, his 37th straight win on a clay court, and a share of third place with Bjorn Borg and Manual Orantes on the list of players with the most titles on clay. Indeed, Monte Carlo has been very good to Rafa. He has not lost there since 2003.

The next few tournaments had up and down moments for Rafa. He would win his sixth Barcelona Title by defeating Ferrer in the finals, becoming the first man in the Open Era to win two tournaments at least six times each. At Madrid, he would defeat Federer but lose to Djokovic in the finals, and then go on to win the French Open by defeating Federer for the title.

Rafa played well at Wimbledon until he met Djokovic in the finals. Rafa lost the first two sets, won the third, and lost the fourth set. Djokovic shot past Rafa in the world rankings and placed himself at the number one spot, with Rafa at number two spot. This was the first time since 2004 that neither Rafa nor Federer held the number one spot. It also ended Rafa's winning streak in Grand Slam finals at seven, thus preventing him from tying Pete Sampra's record of eight. This also marked the first time since 2007 that Rafa had lost at Wimbledon since his five-set loss to Federer that year.

Rafa had to rest his foot for a month due to an injury he suffered at Wimbledon. He would lose the next three tournaments: the Rogers Cup to Ivan Dodig, the Cincinnati Masters to Mardy Fish, and the U.S. Open to Novak Djokovic. During a post-match press conference after his victory over David Nalbandian at the U.S. Open, he collapsed from severe cramps prior to facing Novak Djokovic in the finals. Fans and reporters alike were wondering if these cramps had any bearing on his play in the finals with Djokovic. Rafa would never make excuses for his poor play, so we may never know.

Rafa would wrap up the season with losses at the Japan Open Tennis Championships to Andy Murray, the Shanghai Masters at the hands of Florian Mayer, and at the ATP World Tour Finals by Roger Federer in a round-robin. In the following match at the ATP World Tour Finals, Rafa faced Jo-Wilfried Tsonga and was eliminated from the tournament.

He ended the season by playing in an exhibition match not affiliated with the ATP. At the Mubadala World Tennis

Championships, he was defeated by David Ferrer but won third place rights against Federer.

The 2011 season wasn't too pleasant for Rafa. Injuries plagued him, which made him fall to opponents who would normally be defeated; however, Rafa will never make excuses for his lack of play; he will only say that the other person played better than he did. This was a year that tested Rafa's heart—a year when he would prevail within himself if not on the court.

While 2011 wasn't too nice to Rafa, 2012 appears to be looking better for this young tennis stud. He has already won the Monte-Carlo Rolex Masters by defeating Novak Djokovic in the finals, thus snapping a seven straight loss streak to the top-ranked player—a streak that started at the 2011 Indian Wells Tournament.

He also has won the Barcelona Open for the seventh title in eight years. He defeated David Ferrer in the finals to clinch the title once again.

There have been drawbacks for Rafa this year. The hard courts are beginning to take a toll on his injury-prone knee. He lost the Qatar Open to Gael Monfils and the Australian Open to Novak Djokovic in a record-setting 5 hour 53 minute match. He has further fallen to Federer at Indian Wells and was forced to withdraw in Miami due to knee troubles.

As it stands at the time of this writing, he is ranked third in the world rankings, behind Djokovic and Federer. Only time will tell if this proven champion will be able to climb his way back to number one. Either way, it will be fun to watch him for years to come.

"I thought that maybe I needed someone I could in some way identify with. And Rafael Nadal is a person who has been totally committed to his career since he was very young. Since he was 17, I believe."

—Shakira, when asked why she picked Rafa for her music video

Beyond the Court

Rafa's on-court style is well-known throughout the tennis world. He gained in popularity ever since he played his first professional match in 2001. What is Rafa like off the court? Is he the same aggressive, outlandishly spoken person that he appears to be while facing players like Roger Federer or Novak Djokovic? There is no simple answer to that question. He both "is" and "isn't."

Rafa's endorsement deals are as varied as anything you could imagine, from being the face for Armani's underwear advertisements to being the spokesperson for Quely, a chocolate-coated treat manufacturer that he has been eating products from since he was a young boy. By noticing exactly what he endorses with his face, you can see that he only endorses or takes part in products and companies that he uses himself. Thus, he is an athlete who has not sold out to corporate sponsors. He keeps himself grounded and knows who he is. He will not change himself for mere money.

He not only conducts business for the sake of endorsements, either. He has been featured in Shakira's music video, "Gypsy," and even has his name in the stars—quite literally, the stars. There is a main belt asteroid discovered in 2003 at the Observatorio Astronomico de Mallorca, Spain It was named 128036 Rafaelnadal, after Rafael Nadal! This proves that his tennis talents have outreached the earth and into the far reaches of space.

Not steering too far from his love of another sport, Rafa has reportedly purchased a 10% stake in the soccer team Real Madrid. His move to buy a share in the team has helped the club with their debt crisis and allows him his childhood dream of following his team wherever they play. The club even offered him the role of Vice President, which he turned down. He is also a strong supporter of the Spanish National Team and is only one of six people not affiliated with the team to be allowed into the locker room after Spain's victory during the 2010 FIFA World Cup Final.

Rafa's interests go beyond sports. He has planted trees in Thailand for the Million Trees for the King project and has even started the Fundación Rafa Nadal, which focuses on social work and developmental aid to children in Mallorca, Spain.

His foundation is focusing on Spain as of right now, but has hopes to help across the world in the poorest of places. He traveled to India in 2010 to transform one of the poorest and most needy areas in the land, and has an academy in the state of Andhra Pradesh to help educate its people.

Although he stays grounded to his hometown, he does enjoy the fruits of all his hard labor and training. He owns an Aston Martin DBS, which he can be seen driving around the streets of Manacor, Mallorca, where he still lives in a five-story apartment building with his mother, father and younger sister. In June 2009, it was reported that his mother and father, Ana Maria and Sebastian, had separated. Fans speculated throughout internet message boards that this was the reason for Rafa's setback from 2009-2011.

When he was younger, Nadal would rush home from school to watch his favorite Dragon Ball cartoon character, Goku, on the television. He has been compared to the legendary cartoon character, since Goku is from another world. It has been said that Rafa is the "Goku of the tennis courts" due to his otherworldly playing style and unbelievable returns.

He has been dating his girlfriend, Maria Francisca Perello, since 2005 and he enjoys playing golf and soccer when not on the tennis court. Truly a well-rounded individual, Rafa will have a place in tennis history and lore. He is a special player, and one we should watch for many more years.

Printed in the USA
CPSIA information can be obtained
at www.ICGtesting.com
CBHW051530051124
16948CB00033B/1019